W9-ABR-210

BEST
EDITORIAL
CARTOONS
OF THE YEAR

ED HALL
Courtesy Baker County Press (Fla.)

BEST EDITORIAL CARTOONS OF THE YEAR

2009 EDITION

Edited by
CHARLES BROOKS

PELICAN PUBLISHING COMPANY
GRETNA 2009

Copyright © 2009
By Charles Brooks
All rights reserved

The cartoons in this volume are produced with the expressed
permission of the individual cartoonists and their respective
publications and/or syndicates. Any unauthorized
publication or use is strictly prohibited.

Library of Congress Serial Catalog Data

Best Editorial Cartoons, 1972-
Gretna [La.] Pelican Pub. Co.
v. 37 cm annual—
"A pictorial history of the year."

United States—Politics and Government—
1969—Caricatures and cartoons—Periodicals.
E839.5.B45 320.9'7309240207 73-643645
ISSN 0091-2220   MARC-S

Printed in the United States of America

Published by Pelican Publishing Company, Inc.
1000 Burmaster Street, Gretna, Louisiana 70053

Contents

Award-Winning Cartoons

2008 PULITZER PRIZE

MICHAEL RAMIREZ

Editorial Cartoonist
Investors Business Daily

Born in Tokyo, Japan; graduate of the University of California at Irvine, 1984; former editorial cartoonist for the *Newport Ensign,* the *San Clemente Daily Sun* and *Post,* the *Memphis Commercial Appeal,* and the *Los Angeles Times;* presently editorial cartoonist and editorial page co-editor of *Investors Business Daily;* previous winner of the Pulitzer Prize for editorial cartooning, 1994, the Sigma Delta Chi Award (three times), the National Journalism Award, the John Fischetti Award, and the H.L. Mencken Award; cartoons syndicated by Copley News Service to more than 550 newspapers and magazines.

2007 SIGMA DELTA CHI AWARD
(Awarded in 2008)

MICHAEL RAMIREZ

Editorial Cartoonist
Investors Business Daily

2007 JOHN FISCHETTI AWARD

(Awarded in 2008)

MICHAEL RAMIREZ

Editorial Cartoonist

Investors Business Daily

MIKE PETERS

Editorial Cartoonist
Dayton Daily News

Born October 9, 1943, in St. Louis, Missouri; earned degree in fine arts from Washington University, 1965; served with the U.S. Army as an artist in Okinawa; began career with the *Chicago Daily News;* editorial cartoonist for the *Dayton Daily News,* 1969 to the present; draws popular comic strip "Mother Goose" and "Grimm"; winner of the Pulitzer Prize, 1981, and the Overseas Press Club Award, 1990; awarded honorary Doctor of Humane Letters degree by the University of Dayton, 1998; popular lecturer at colleges on political topics; cartoons syndicated in more than 400 newspapers.

2008 OVERSEAS PRESS CLUB AWARD

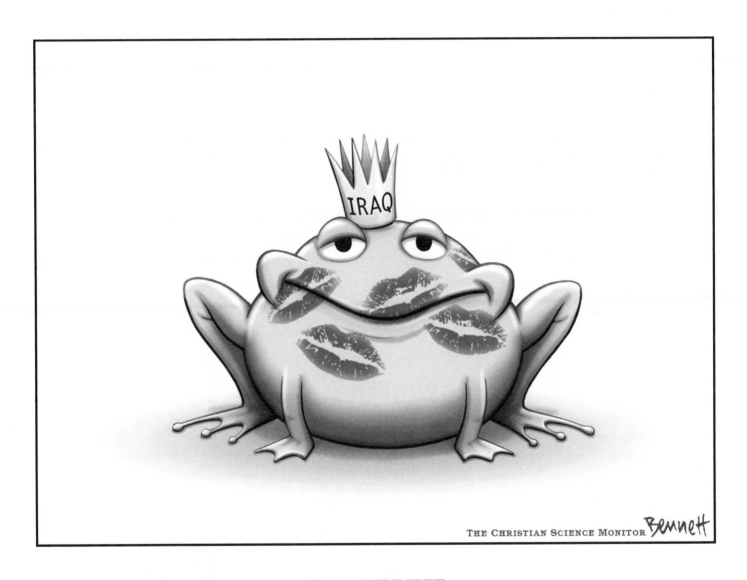

THE CHRISTIAN SCIENCE MONITOR *Bennett*

CLAY BENNETT

Editorial Cartoonist
Christian Science Monitor

Born January 20, 1958, in Clinton, South Carolina; graduated from the University of North Alabama, 1980; staff artist and editorial cartoonist for the *Pittsburgh Post-Gazette* and the *Fayetteville (N.C.) Times* before joining the *St. Petersburg Times* in 1981; editorial cartoonist for the *Christian Science Monitor* (where the above prize-winning cartoon appeared), 1998-2008, and the *Chattanooga Times-Free Press,* 2008 to the present; previous winner of the Overseas Press Club Award, 2005; winner of the Pulitzer Prize, 2002, the Sigma Delta Chi Award, 2001, the John Fischetti Award, 2001 and 2005, and the National Headliner Award, 1999, 2000, and 2004; past president of the Association of American Editorial Cartoonists.

2007 SCRIPPS HOWARD AWARD

(Awarded in 2008)

STEVE KELLEY

Editorial Cartoonist
The Times-Picayune

Born in Richmond, Virginia, 1959; graduated from Dartmouth College, 1981; editorial cartoonist for the *San Diego Union-Tribune,* 1981-2001, and the *New Orleans Times-Picayune,* 2002 to the present; winner of the National Headliner Award, 2001; Montgomery Fellow at Dartmouth College, 2008; cartoons distributed by Creators Syndicate.

2008 HERBLOCK AWARD

JOHN SHERFFIUS

Editorial Cartoonist
Boulder (Colo.) Camera

Began drawing editorial cartoons while in college for the UCLA *Daily Bruin;* work published regularly in the *Boulder Camera;* winner of the Sigma Delta Chi Award, the National Press Foundation's Berryman Award, the Scripps Howard National Journalism Award, and the Robert F. Kennedy Journalism Award; cartoons distributed nationally by Creators Syndicate.

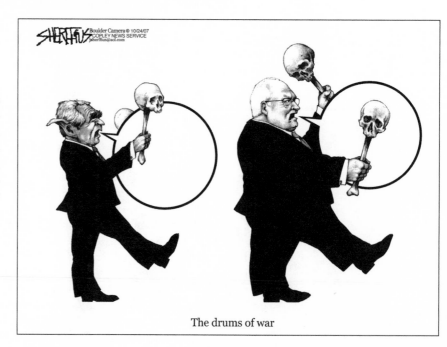

The drums of war

BEST
EDITORIAL
CARTOONS
OF THE YEAR

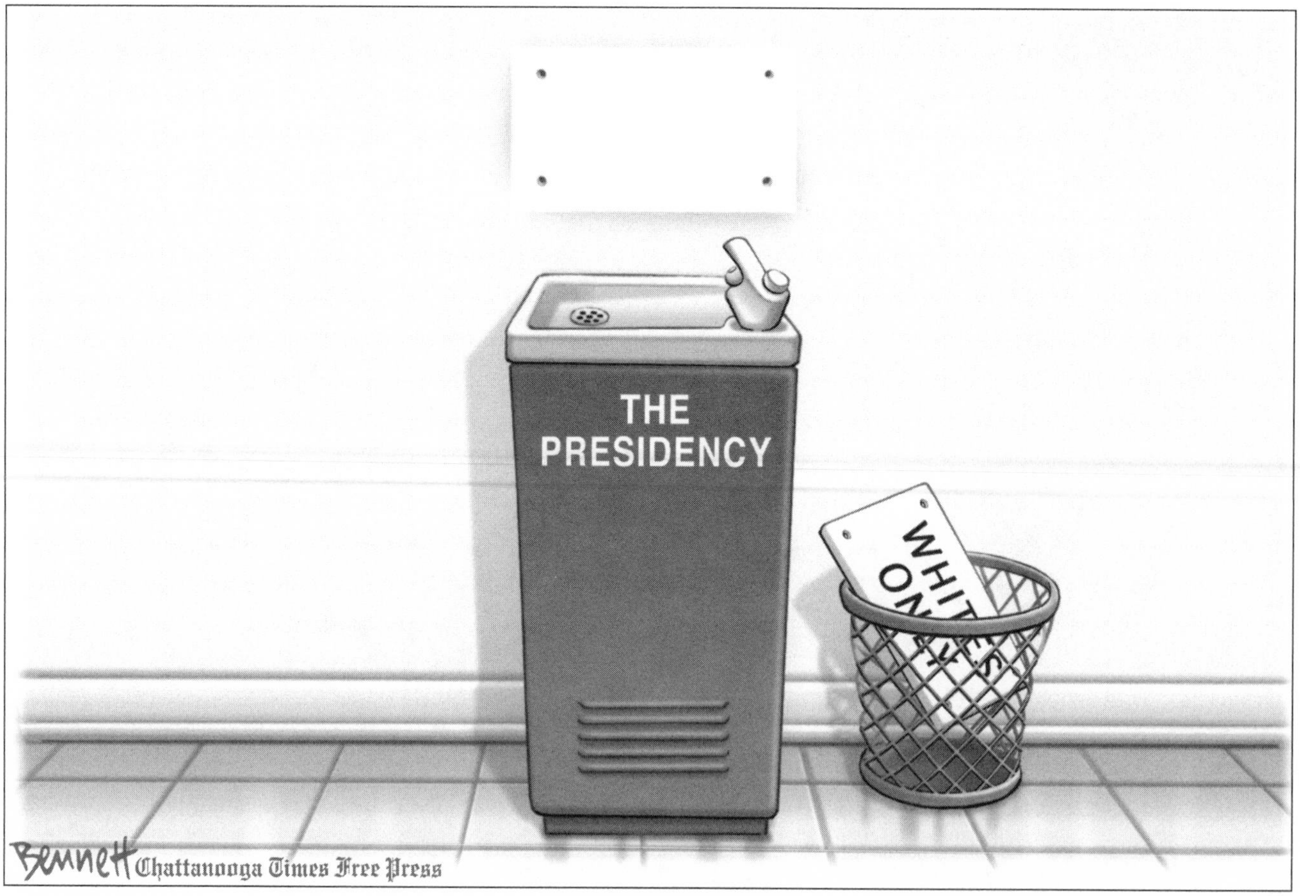
THE PRESIDENCY
WHITES ONLY
Bennett Chattanooga Times Free Press

CLAY BENNETT
Courtesy Chattanooga Times Free Press

DICK LOCHER
Courtesy Chicago Tribune

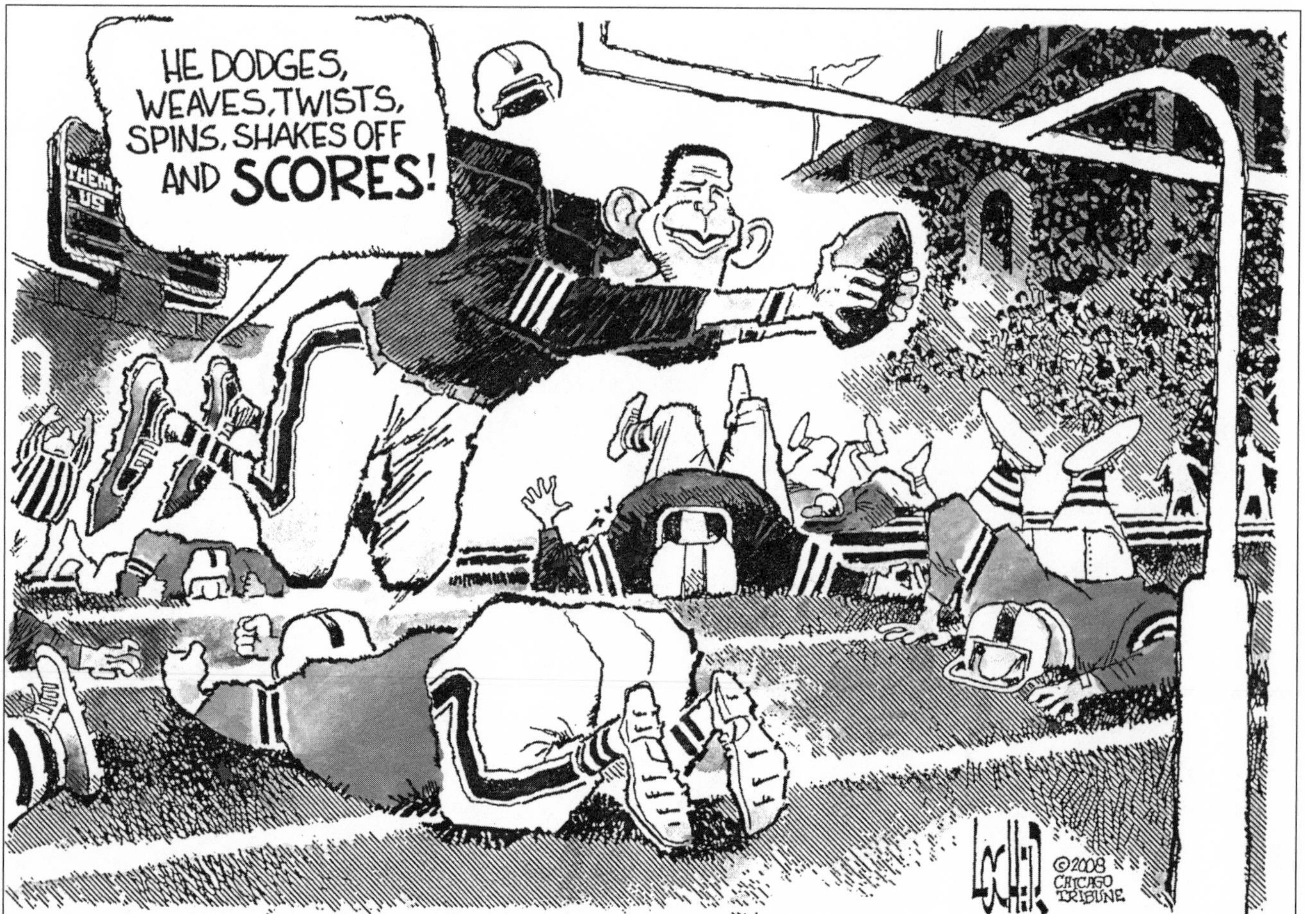
HE DODGES, WEAVES, TWISTS, SPINS, SHAKES OFF AND SCORES!
THEM
US
LOCHER ©2008 CHICAGO TRIBUNE

The Winner!

Barack Obama, a 47-year-old Democratic senator from Illinois, was elected America's first black president, handily defeating Republican Sen. John McCain in the November 4 election.

Obama, who campaigned on a platform of change, had taken a commanding lead in national polls in September after a near-collapse of the stock market and a tidal wave of mortgage foreclosures. The Democrats were successful in tying McCain to the hugely unpopular President George Bush, whose approval rating sank below 30 percent.

The Republicans, on the other hand, attempted to paint Obama as a tax-and-spend radical bent on transforming American society and redistributing the wealth.

After almost eight years of President Bush, the nation's voters had signaled they were ready for something—perhaps anything—different.

CHRIS BRITT
Courtesy State Journal-Register (Ill.)

WILLIAM WARREN
Courtesy WARRENTOONS.COM

ROBERT ARIAIL
Courtesy The State (S.C.)

The Presidential Campaign

For the first time, an African-American, Illinois Sen. Barack Obama, won a major party's nomination for president. The Democratic race developed into a shootout between Obama and Sen. Hillary Clinton, with Clinton doggedly remaining in the race to the end.

On the Republican side, Arizona Sen. John McCain prevailed over former Gov. Mitt Romney of Massachusetts, former New York Mayor Rudy Giuliani, former Gov. Mike Huckabee of Arkansas, and former Sen. Fred Thompson of Tennessee.

Florida and Michigan violated Democratic Party rules by moving up the dates for their primary elections, and for a time their delegates were threatened with exclusion from the convention.

Sen. Obama carried a lot of heavy political baggage, much of it accumulated working as a community organizer in Chicago. *New Yorker* magazine drew fire for caricaturing the Obamas on its cover, portraying the senator as a Muslim and his wife as an angry black militant. Obama, sporting a pencil-thin resume in foreign affairs, picked Delaware Sen. Joe Biden, a 35-year veteran of Congress, as his running mate, while McCain shocked just about everyone by choosing a relative newcomer to the national stage, Alaska Gov. Sarah Palin.

JIM BORGMAN
Courtesy Cincinnati Enquirer

GARY VARVEL
Courtesy Indianapolis Star

NORTHEAST TEXAS COMMUNITY COLLEGE
LEARNING RESOURCE CENTER
MT. PLEASANT, TEXAS 75455

19

RON ROGERS
Courtesy South Bend Tribune

JUSTIN DeFREITAS
Courtesy Berkeley Daily Planet

MIKE PETERS
Courtesy Dayton Daily News

WILLIAM WARREN
Courtesy WARRENTOONS.COM

WALT HANDELSMAN
Courtesy Newsday

JAKE FULLER
Courtesy Gainesville Sun

MIKE KEEFE
Courtesy Denver Post

MICHAEL RAMIREZ
Courtesy Investors Business Daily

TIM JACKSON
Courtesy Chicago Defender

SAGE STOSSEL
Courtesy The Atlantic Monthly

GRAEME MACKAY
Courtesy Hamilton Spectator (Canada)

BARRY HUNAU
Courtesy cartoonsbybarry.com

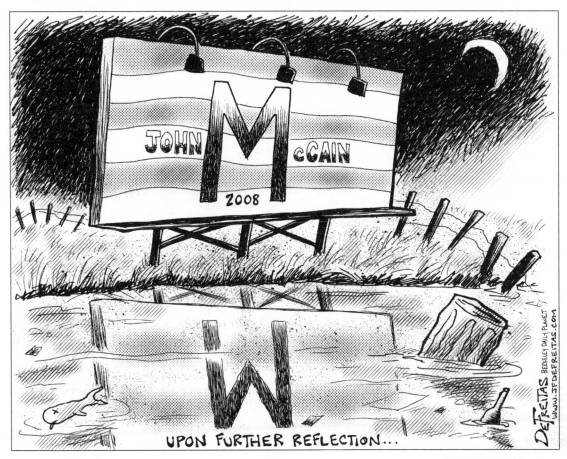

JUSTIN DeFREITAS
Courtesy Berkeley Daily Planet

STEVE GREENBERG
Courtesy Ventura County Star

25

ROGER HARVELL
Courtesy Arkansas Democrat-Gazette

JOHN SHERFFIUS
Courtesy Boulder Camera (Colo.)

"My friends, let's finish the job!"

NICK ANDERSON
Courtesy Houston Chronicle

WILLIAM WARREN
Courtesy WARRENTOONS.COM

27

PAUL COMBS
Courtesy Tribune Media Services

CHRIS WRIGHT
Courtesy wright4u@comcast.net

SCOTT-ALLEN PIERSON
Courtesy Viking News (N.J.)

RICK McKEE
Courtesy Augusta Chronicle (Ga.)

STEVE BREEN
Courtesy San Diego Union-Tribune

29

ROB ROGERS
Courtesy Pittsburgh Post-Gazette

JIM BORGMAN
Courtesy Cincinnati Enquirer

WAYNE STAYSKAL
Courtesy Tribune Media Services

J.R. ROSE
Courtesy Byrd Newspapers of Virginia

FRED SEBASTIAN
Courtesy Artizans Syndicate

JACK HIGGINS
Courtesy Chicago Sun-Times

JOHN DEERING
Courtesy Arkansas Democrat-Gazette

JACK HIGGINS
Courtesy Chicago Sun-Times

CHARLES DANIEL
Courtesy Knoxville News-Sentinel

33

THEO MOUDAKIS
Courtesy Toronto Star

JON RICHARDS
Courtesy Albuquerque Journal North

STEVE KELLEY
Courtesy The Times-Picayune (La.)

DAN FITZGERALD
Courtesy Louisville Courier-Journal

ROB SMITH, JR.
Courtesy DBR Media

JESSE SPRINGER
Courtesy Eugene Register-Guard (Ore.)

GEORGE DANBY
Courtesy Bangor Daily News

JEFF PARKER
Courtesy Florida Today

JOHN RILEY
Courtesy johnrileycartoons.com

STEVE McBRIDE
Courtesy Independence Daily Reporter (Kan.)

JOHN BRANCH
Courtesy San Antonio Express-News

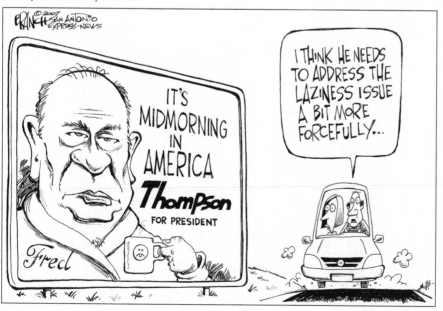

RICK KOLLINGER
Courtesy the Star Democrat (Md.)

ED GAMBLE
Courtesy Florida Times-Union

DICK LOCHER
Courtesy Chicago Tribune

JIM MORIN
Courtesy Miami Herald

JIM BORGMAN
Courtesy Cincinnati Enquirer

SCOTT COFFMAN
Courtesy Scott Coffman

41

TOM BECK
Courtesy Freeport Journal-Standard (Ill.)

JOHN COLE
Courtesy Scranton Times-Tribune

PAUL CONRAD
Courtesy Tribune Media Services

ED STEIN
Courtesy Rocky Mountain News (Colo.)

NEIL GRAHAME
Courtesy Spencer Newspapers

The name-dropping begins...

"Of course I clearly remember meeting the Pope for the first time. The plane was circling to avoid sniper fire and we ran with our heads down to the Vatican..."

CHARLIE HALL
Courtesy Rhode Island News Group

RICK McKEE
Courtesy Augusta Chronicle (Ga.)

DANA SUMMERS
Courtesy Orlando Sentinel

THE DOMINATED   THE NOMINATED

TED RALL
Courtesy Universal Press Syndicate

BRUCE MacKINNON
Courtesy Halifax Herald (Canada)

JERRY BARNETT
Courtesy Boonville Standard (Ind.)

WALT HANDELSMAN
Courtesy Newsday

BOB ENGLEHART
Courtesy Hartford Courant

47

...AND MY RECENT PRIMARY PERFORMANCES PROVE...

DEAN TURNBLOOM
Courtesy editorialcartoonists.com

CARL MOORE
Courtesy Creators Syndicate

JESSE SPRINGER
Courtesy Eugene Register-Guard (Ore.)

MIKE LESTER
Courtesy Rome News-Tribune (Ga.)

J.D. CROWE
Courtesy Mobile Press-Register

CHAN LOWE
Courtesy Fort Lauderdale News/
South Florida Sun Sentinel

DAN FITZGERALD
Courtesy Louisville Courier-Journal

Governor Palin

Republican presidential candidate Sen. John McCain rocked the political world when he named as his vice-presidential running mate the 44-year-old gun-toting, pro-life governor of Alaska, Sarah Palin. Critics immediately pounced, ridiculing her candidacy, her family, her lack of experience on the national scene, her participation in a beauty pageant 25 years ago, even her self-proclaimed ability to shoot and carve a moose.

But Republicans weren't listening. Her selection immediately energized what had been a less than enthusiastic party base, and campaign donations and pledges of support began to roll in.

Palin, the mother of five who once served as mayor of the small town of Wasilla, Alaska, brought with her a reputation as a hard-nosed, no-nonsense reformer and a staunch defender of family values.

ED GAMBLE
Courtesy Florida Times-Union

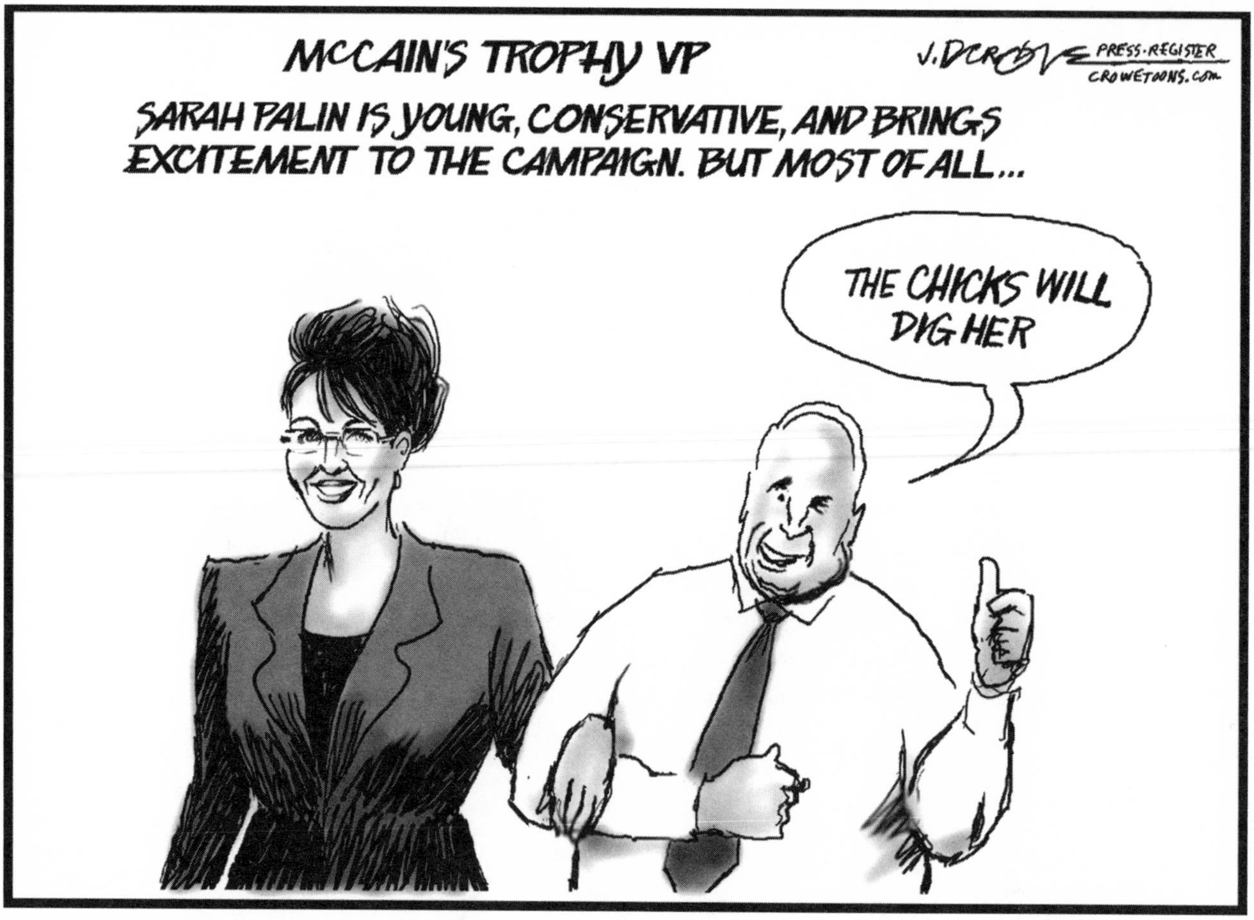
MᶜCAIN'S TROPHY VP
J. D. CROWE PRESS-REGISTER crowetoons.com
SARAH PALIN IS YOUNG, CONSERVATIVE, AND BRINGS EXCITEMENT TO THE CAMPAIGN. BUT MOST OF ALL...
THE CHICKS WILL DIG HER

J.D. CROWE
Courtesy Mobile Press-Register

DOUGLAS MacGREGOR
Courtesy Fort Myers News-Press

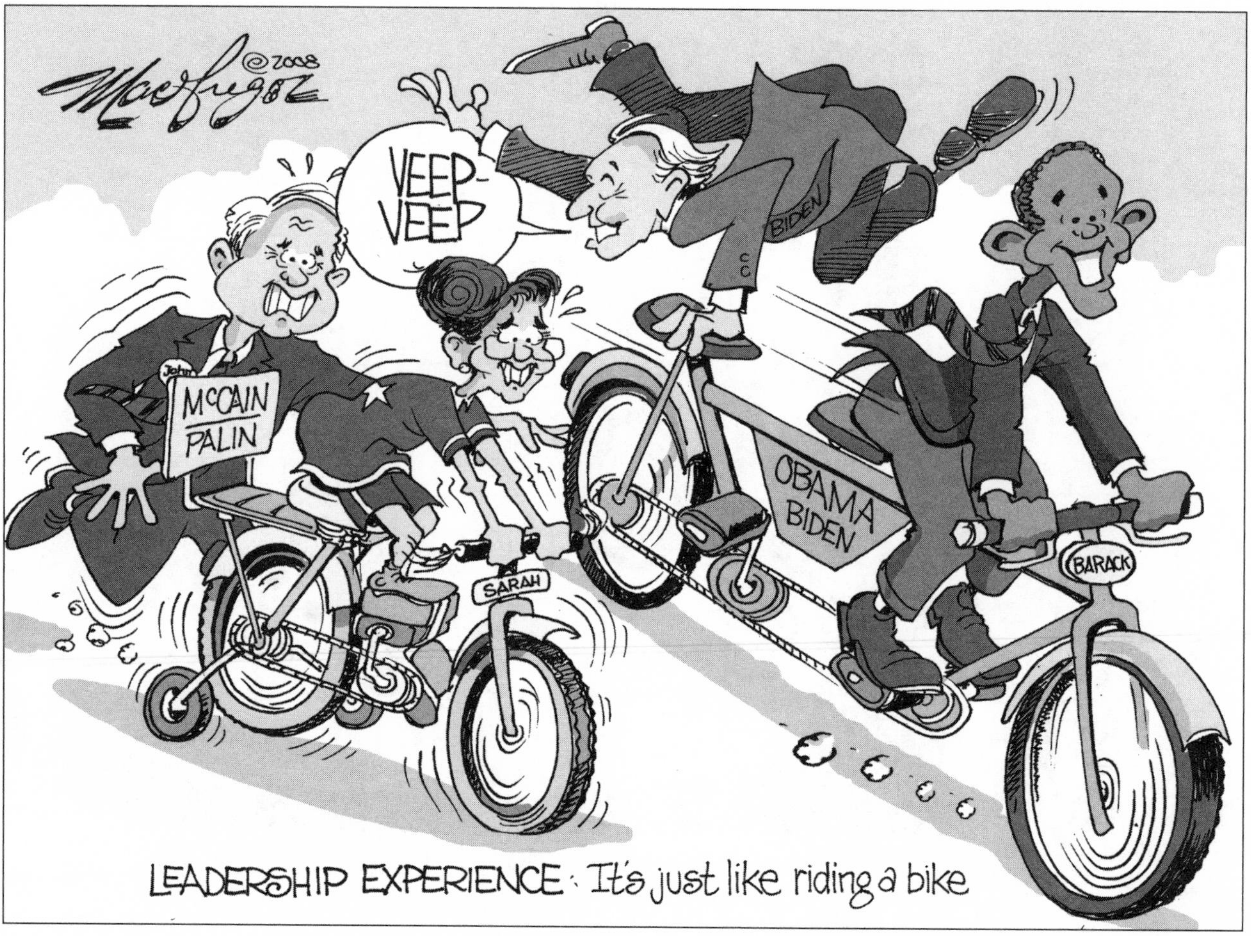
MacGregor ©2008
VEEP-VEEP
BIDEN
John
MᶜCAIN PALIN
SARAH
OBAMA BIDEN
BARACK
LEADERSHIP EXPERIENCE: It's just like riding a bike

ROY PETERSON
Courtesy Vancouver Sun

BOB LANG
Courtesy Rightoons.com

SCOTT STANTIS
Courtesy Birmingham News

ROY PETERSON
Courtesy Vancouver Sun

MIKE KEEFE
Courtesy Denver Post

BILL GARNER
Courtesy Washington Times

ROB TORNOE
Courtesy rob.tornoe@potlicker.com

STEVE LINDSTROM
Courtesy Duluth News-Tribune

JAKE FULLER
Courtesy Gainesville Sun

BILL GARNER
Courtesy Washington Times

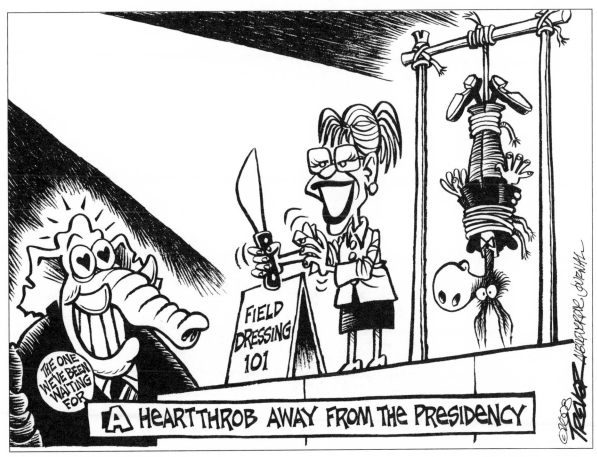

JOHN TREVER
Courtesy Albuquerque Journal

GARY MARKSTEIN
Courtesy Creators News Service

57

MICHAEL RAMIREZ
Courtesy Investors Business Daily

RICHARD CROWSON
Courtesy Wichita Eagle

Bill Clinton

Former President Bill Clinton took to the presidential campaign trail in 2008 to promote the candidacy of his wife, Hillary. It was not always smooth sailing, and a debate soon arose over whether his efforts were helping or hindering her cause.

In the days leading up to the Democratic primary in South Carolina, he accused her opponents of "playing the race card," angering many Democrats and African-American voters. In other campaign appearances, he seemed as interested in talking about himself and his tenure as president as he was in boosting Hillary's candidacy.

Nevertheless, after his wife was eliminated from the race, he announced he would do everything possible to further Barack Obama's candidacy. He later appeared at a number of rallies praising Obama.

ROBERT ARIAIL
Courtesy The State (S.C.)

JIM MORIN
Courtesy Miami Herald

TOM STIGLICH
Courtesy Northeast Times (Pa.)

LUCAS TURNBLOOM
Courtesy Artizans.com

CHAN LOWE
Courtesy Fort Lauderdale News/
South Florida Sun Sentinel

GRAEME MACKAY
Courtesy Hamilton Spectator (Canada)

THEO MOUDAKIS
Courtesy Toronto Star

ROB TORNOE
Courtesy rob.tornoe@potlicker.com

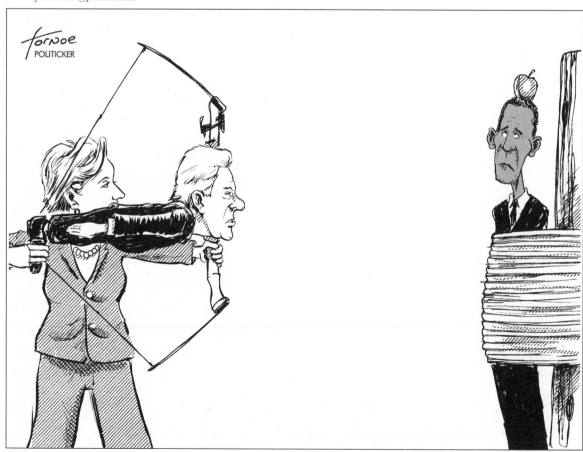

PAUL COMBS
Courtesy Tribune Media Services

CHARLES DANIEL
Courtesy Knoxville News-Sentinel

MIKE LUCKOVICH
Courtesy Atlanta Journal-Constitution

CHRIS BRITT
Courtesy State Journal-Register (Ill.)

The Reverend Wright

"Inflammatory rhetoric" by the Rev. Jeremiah Wright, pastor of the 10,000-member Trinity United Church of Christ in Chicago attended by the Obama family, created a raft of problems for the Obama campaign.

The Democratic nominee eventually resigned from the church, where he had worshipped for some 20 years, after some of Wright's remarks came to light. Among other things, the clergyman declared that America was responsible for 9/11, for the AIDS epidemic, and for spreading terrorism around the world.

Furthermore, America was an awful nation, a racist society to its core. It was Wright's racist declarations that bothered most Americans, who wondered how the candidate could have listened to his pastor's sermons of hate for 20 years.

At first, Obama dismissed the furor over Wright's statements, comparing them to the rants of "an old uncle who says things I don't always agree with." But when Wright accused him of political posturing, Obama found the reverend's words "outrageous and destructive" and resigned from the church.

J.R. ROSE
Courtesy Byrd Newspapers of Virginia

DAVID DONAR
Courtesy Macomb Daily (Miss.)

RANDY BISH
Courtesy Tribune-Review (Pa.)

DAVID BROWN
Courtesy Los Angeles Sentinel

JIM HUNT
Courtesy Charlotte Post

FRED SEBASTIAN
Courtesy Artizans Syndicate

Reverend Wright: "the Lord listens and heeds our call"
Barack Obama: "apparently not; you're still here"

DENNIS GALVEZ
Courtesy Philippine News

GARY MARKSTEIN
Courtesy Creators News Service

The Bush Administration

President George Bush's popular support hovered around the 30 percent mark for much of the year, but the rating of Congress plummeted even lower—to 10 percent in one poll. Opting to send more troops to Iraq—the so-called surge—carried grave risks for the President, but seemed to have paid off. By midyear, according to Gen. David Petraeus, violence was dramatically down throughout the country.

In a 5-4 decision, the Supreme Court ruled that the Military Commissions Act of 2006 was unconstitutional because it purported to abolish the writ of habeas corpus, the means by which a detainee can challenge his detention.

Bush sought legislation granting legal immunity to telecommunications companies that aided in the surveillance of suspected terrorists. The measure was blocked by Democrats. Speaker Nancy Pelosi maintained she was trying to balance concerns about civil liberties against the government's spy powers.

A book by former White House spokesman Scott McClellan was sharply critical of President Bush. The economy continued to suffer because of the war, out of control gasoline prices, and the collapse of many financial institutions.

NATE BEELER
Courtesy Washington Examiner

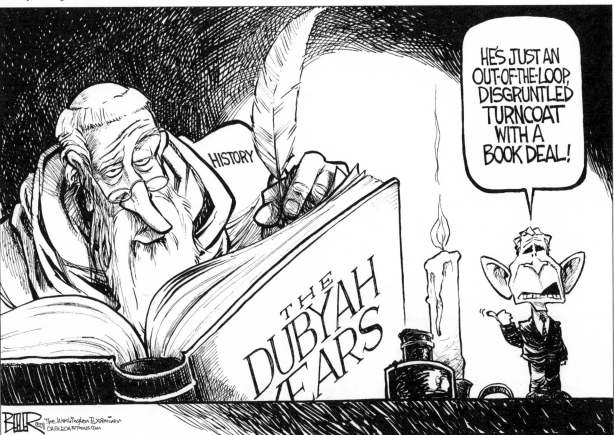

DICK LOCHER
Courtesy Chicago Tribune

JOHN BRANCH
Courtesy San Antonio Express-News

ED STEIN
Courtesy Rocky Mountain News (Colo.)

RON ROGERS
Courtesy South Bend Tribune

MIKE PETERS
Courtesy Dayton Daily News

JIMMY MARGULIES
Courtesy The Record (N.J.)

MILT PRIGGEE
Courtesy Puget Sound Business Journal

POL GALVEZ
Courtesy Philippine News

JERRY BARNETT
Courtesy Boonville Standard (Ind.)

WASHINGTON

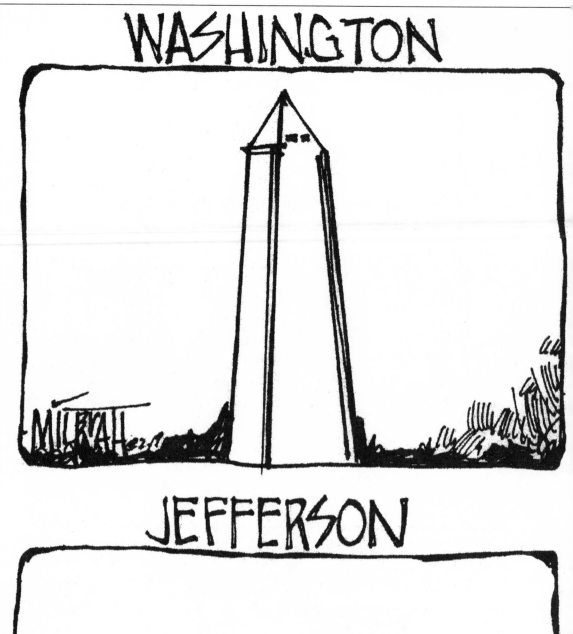

JEFFERSON

DEB MILBRATH
Courtesy CNN AAEC Website

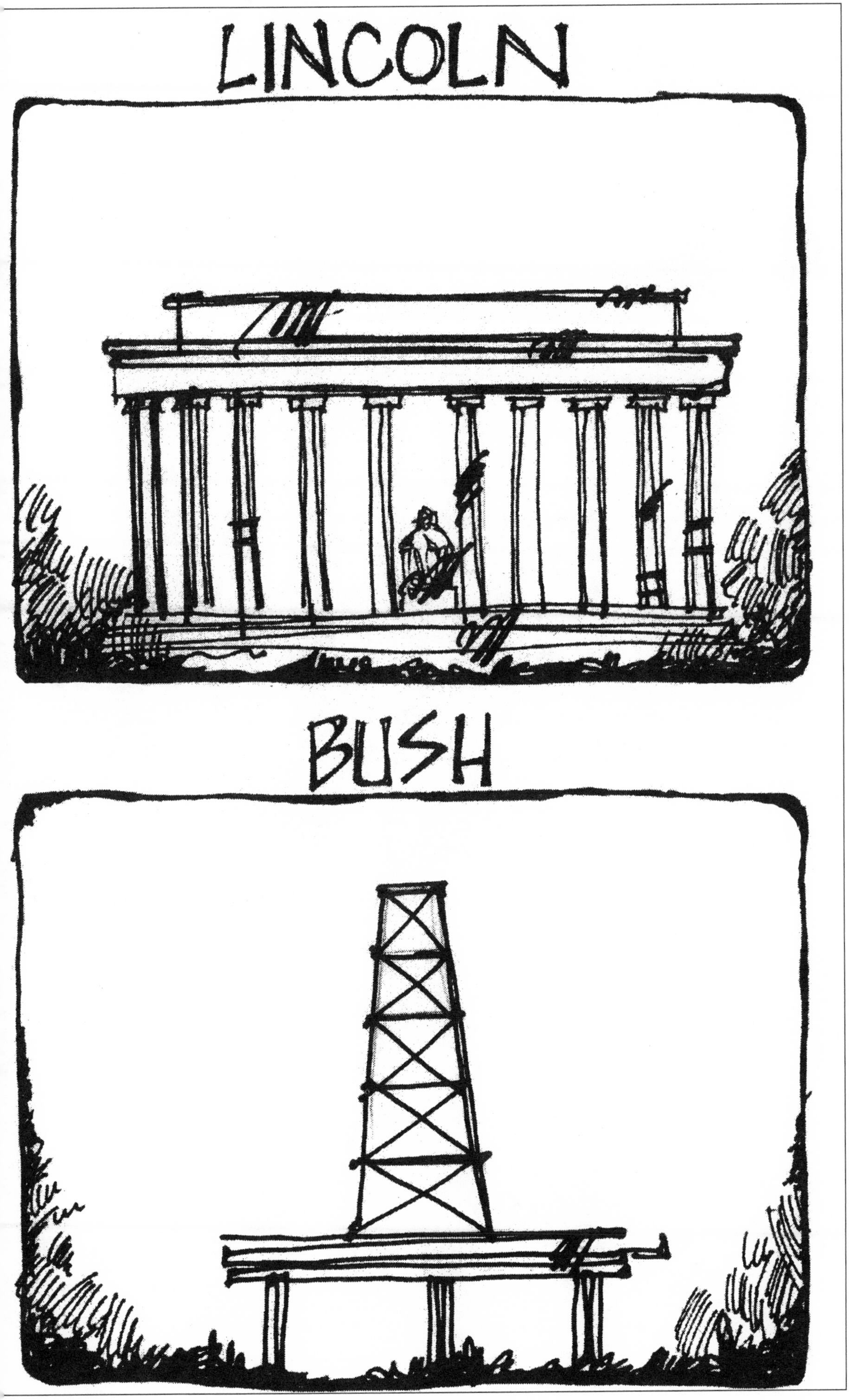
LINCOLN
BUSH

THE END OF AN ERA: BUSH AND CHENEY

PAUL CONRAD
Courtesy Tribune Media Services

JOHN COLE
Courtesy Scranton Times-Tribune

RICHARD BARTHOLOMEW
Courtesy ARTIZANS.COM

NEWS ITEM: PRESIDENT BUSH SAYS HE GAVE UP GOLF OUT OF RESPECT FOR U.S. TROOPS IN IRAQ.

..AN' LET ME TELL YOU— MY HANDICAP HAS GONE ALL TO HECK...

MIKE PETERS
Courtesy Dayton Daily News

ROB TORNOE
Courtesy rob.tornoe@potlicker.com

News Item: Bush: 'Gas at four dollars a gallon? I hadn't heard that.'

GERALD GARDEN
Courtesy Garden ARToons

JIM SIERGEY
Courtesy jimsiergey.com

JON RICHARDS
Courtesy Albuquerque Journal North

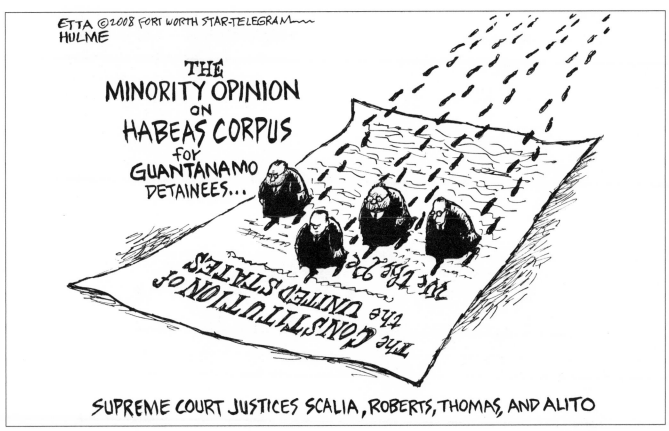

ETTA HULME
Courtesy Fort Worth Star-Telegram

CLAY BENNETT
Courtesy Chattanooga Times Free Press

JOE R. LANE
Courtesy editorialcartoonists.com

ROB ROGERS
Courtesy Pittsburgh Post-Gazette

80

GRAEME MACKAY
Courtesy Hamilton Spectator (Canada)

JOHN DEERING
Courtesy Arkansas Democrat-Gazette

PAUL CONRAD
Courtesy Tribune Media Services

MICHAEL POHRER
Courtesy National Free Press (Mo.)

MIKE KEEFE
Courtesy Denver Post

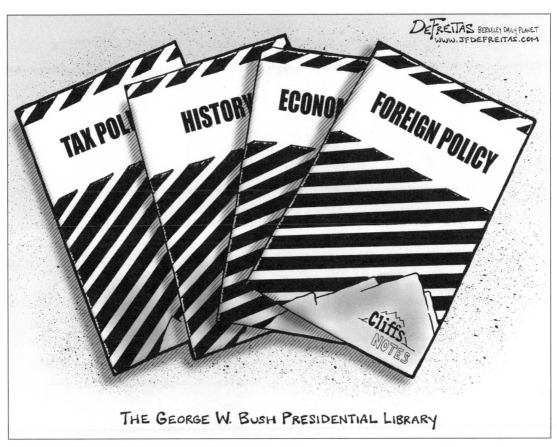

JUSTIN DeFREITAS
Courtesy Berkeley Daily Planet

MIKE LUCKOVICH
Courtesy Atlanta Journal-Constitution

MIKE LUCKOVICH
Courtesy Atlanta Journal-Constitution

HAP PITKIN
Courtesy Boulder Daily Camera (Colo.)

The Economy

Stocks tumbled in 2008 as investors focused on cascading problems at mortgage companies and watched oil prices climb to $147 per barrel. The Dow Jones Industrial Average recorded wild swings of several hundred points a day as home foreclosures mounted and credit threatened to dry up. But as the market continued its freefall, oil prices suddenly reversed course, quickly dropping to near $60 a barrel.

Employers slashed jobs, and hundreds of thousands of workers dropped out of the labor force. Unemployment shot above 6 percent.

The Federal Reserve announced it would rescue insurance giant American International Group with an emergency $85 billion loan. Earlier, the administration had taken over the quasi-governmental mortgage giants Fannie Mae and Freddie Mac, created by Congress to provide affordable home loans. Lehman Brothers, the country's fourth-largest investment bank and on the verge of bankruptcy, was taken over by Bank of America.

In a desperate attempt to stem the tide, Congress approved a $700 billion bailout to deal with what former Federal Reserve Chairman Alan Greenspan called "a once-in-a-century credit tsunami."

President Bush lifted the ban on offshore drilling.

STEVE LINDSTROM
Courtesy Duluth News-Tribune

85

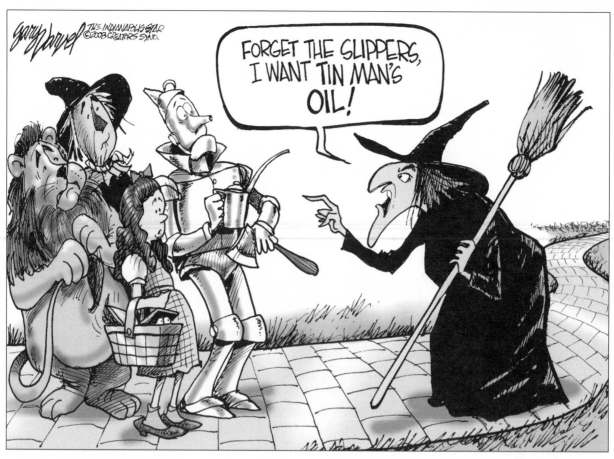

GARY VARVEL
Courtesy Indianapolis Star

TED RALL
Courtesy Universal Press Syndicate

KARL WIMER
Courtesy Denver Business Journal

ROGER SCHILLERSTROM
Courtesy Crain Communications

RICHARD CROWSON
Courtesy Wichita Eagle

PETER EVANS
Courtesy The Islander News (Fla.)

DANA SUMMERS
Courtesy Orlando Sentinel

ROBERT ARIAIL
Courtesy The State (S.C.)

ED GAMBLE
Courtesy Florida Times-Union

DEAN TURNBLOOM
Courtesy editorialcartoonists.com

DON LANDGREN, JR.
Courtesy The Landmark (Mass.)

ROBERT UNELL
Courtesy Kansas City Star

90

DICK LOCHER
Courtesy Chicago Tribune

NATE BEELER
Courtesy Washington Examiner

CHARLES DANIEL
Courtesy Knoxville News-Sentinel

JIM DYKE
Courtesy Jefferson City News-Tribune (Mo.)

ROGER SCHILLERSTROM
Courtesy Crain Communications

S.W. PARRA
Courtesy Fresno Bee

MICHAEL OSBUN
Courtesy Citrus City Chronicle (Fla.)

WAYNE STROOT
Courtesy Hastings Tribune (Neb.)

JIMMY MARGULIES
Courtesy The Record (N.J.)

RON ROGERS
Courtesy South Bend Tribune

DICK LOCHER
Courtesy Chicago Tribune

ROSS GOSSE
Courtesy Editoons.iNCk

STEVE BREEN
Courtesy San Diego Union-Tribune

LARRY WRIGHT
Courtesy Detroit News

STEVE McBRIDE
Courtesy Independence Daily Reporter (Kan.)

ROBERT ARIAIL
Courtesy The State (S.C.)

RICHARD CROWSON
Courtesy Wichita Eagle

JOSEPH HOFFECKER
Courtesy American City Business Journals

JIMMY MARGULIES
Courtesy The Record (N.J.)

GARY MARKSTEIN
Courtesy Creators News Service

NICK ANDERSON
Courtesy Houston Chronicle

99

JEFF PARKER
Courtesy Florida Today

MICHAEL RAMIREZ
Courtesy Investors Business Daily

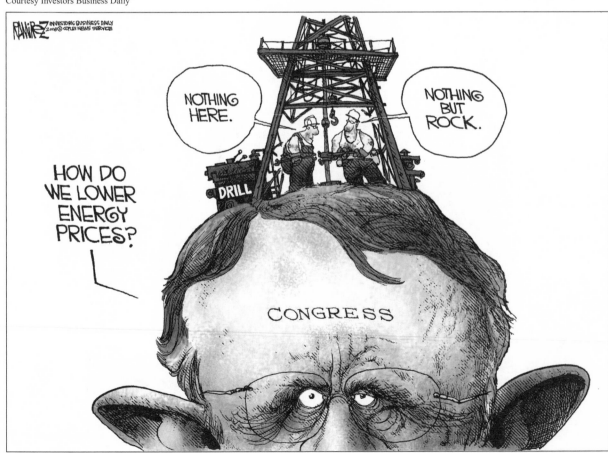

HAP PITKIN
Courtesy Boulder Daily Camera (Colo.)

GENE HERNDON
Courtesy Noblesville Daily Times (Ind.)

ROY PETERSON
Courtesy Vancouver Sun

GEORGE DANBY
Courtesy Bangor Daily News

ROBERT ARIAIL
Courtesy The State (S.C.)

FORECLOSURE

BILL SMITH
Courtesy Lompoc Record (Calif.)

JOE LICCAR
Courtesy Gatehouse Media

TODAY'S VERSION OF THE OLD WOMAN WHO LIVED IN A SHOE.

JERRY BARNETT
Courtesy Boonville Standard (Ind.)

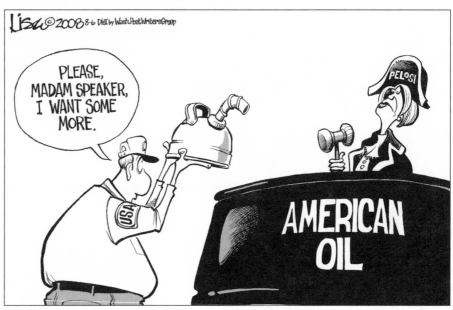

STEPHEN TEMPLETON
Courtesy The Flathead Beacon (Mont.)

LISA BENSON
Courtesy Washington Post Writers Group

WILLIAM FLINT
Courtesy Dallas Morning News

JOSEPH RANK
Courtesy Times-Press-Recorder (Calif.)

DANIEL FENECH
Courtesy Saline Reporter (Mich.)

MICHAEL OSBUN
Courtesy Citrus City Chronicle (Fla.)

ANDREW WAHL
Courtesy Off the Wahl Productions

At Last! Leadership on Wind Power!

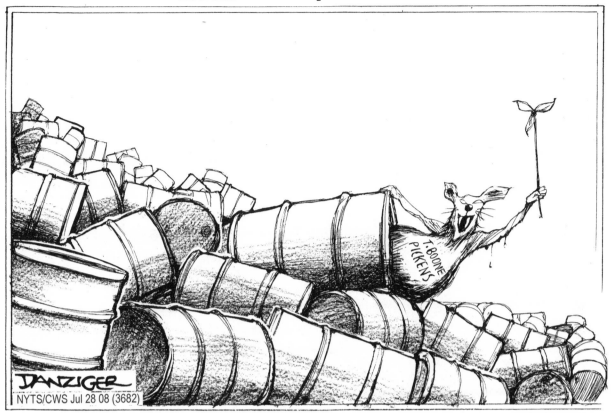

JEFF DANZIGER
Courtesy NYTS/CWS

MIKE LESTER
Courtesy Rome News-Tribune (Ga.)

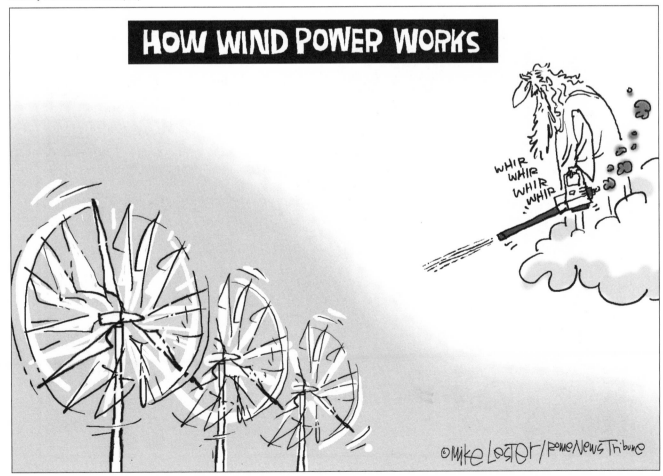

ED HALL
Courtesy Baker County Press (Fla.)

J.D. CROWE
Courtesy Mobile Press-Register

STEVE NEASE
Courtesy Toronto Sun

ROGER SCHILLERSTROM
Courtesy Crain Communications

JIM BUSH
Courtesy Providence Journal (R.I.)

BILL WHITEHEAD
Courtesy Kansas City Business Journal

MILT PRIGGEE
Courtesy Puget Sound Business Journal

Cartoon by Bill Mauldin 1944

JEFF DANZIGER
Courtesy NYTS/CWS

NICK ANDERSON
Courtesy Houston Chronicle

TOM BECK
Courtesy Freeport Journal-Standard (Ill.)

DOUG REGALIA
Courtesy Contra Costa Times (Calif.)

WILLIAM FLINT
Courtesy Dallas Morning News

ROB SMITH, JR.
Courtesy DBR Media

TED RALL
Courtesy Universal Press Syndicate

STEPHEN TEMPLETON
Courtesy The Flathead Beacon (Mont.)

RON ROGERS
Courtesy South Bend Tribune

Foreign Affairs

The Summer Olympics drew attention to several issues, including China's abysmal record on human rights and its choking industrial pollution. Demonstrators focused attention on China's oppression of Tibet and its brutal suppression of dissent at home. Beijing's air quality ranks among the world's most unhealthful. To make matters even worse, the Chinese were accused of using underage gymnasts and of replacing participants deemed "not cute enough."

Many countries rushed aid to Myanmar after a tropical storm killed more than 128,000. Vladimir Putin clung to power and directed the Russian invasion of neighboring Georgia. The attack came after Georgia sought to prevent two breakaway provinces from declaring independence. Meanwhile, the Taliban continued to offer formidable resistance in Afghanistan, and Iran stepped up its nuclear program despite international opposition.

Cuban leader Fidel Castro, stepping down because of failing health, turned over power to his brother, Raul.

Israel celebrated the 60th anniversary of its founding.

PEDRO MOLINA
Courtesy CWS

JOHN DEERING
Courtesy Arkansas Democrat-Gazette

JOHN TREVER
Courtesy Albuquerque Journal

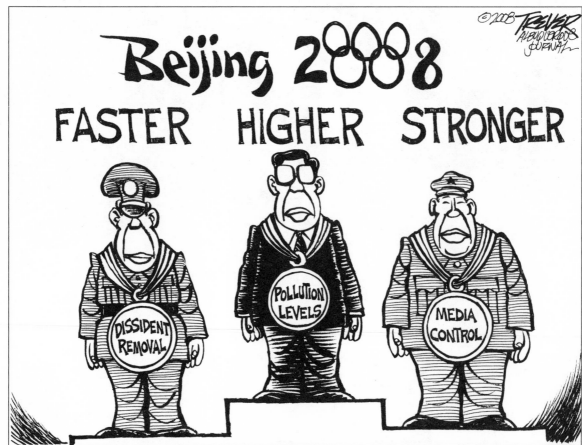

LUCAS TURNBLOOM
Courtesy Artizans.com

ADAM ZYGLIS
Courtesy Buffalo News

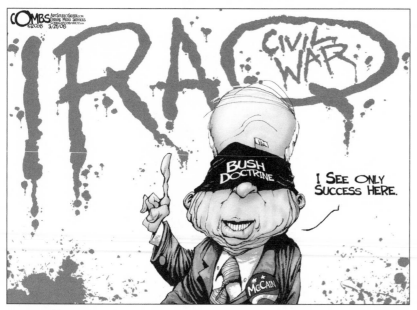

PAUL COMBS
Courtesy Tribune Media Services

JOHN BRANCH
Courtesy San Antonio Express-News

ROSS GOSSE
Courtesy Editoons.iNCk

STEVE NEASE
Courtesy Toronto Sun

JIM BORGMAN
Courtesy Cincinnati Enquirer

SCOTT STANTIS
Courtesy Birmingham News

GLEN STEIN
Courtesy LaPrensa (Fla.)

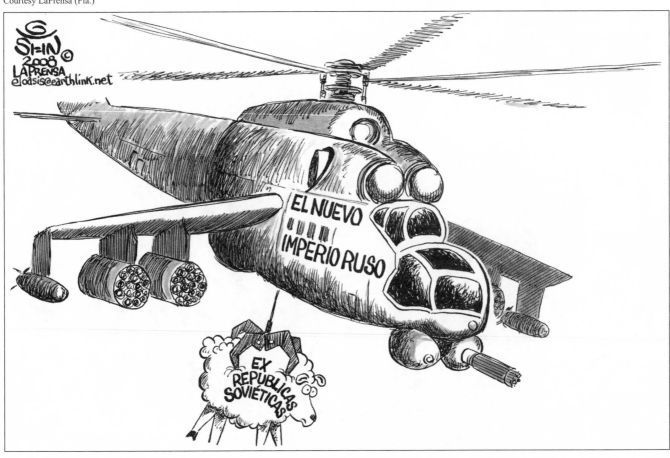

ADAM ZYGLIS
Courtesy Buffalo News

LISA BENSON
Courtesy Washington Post Writers Group

STEVE LINDSTROM
Courtesy Duluth News-Tribune

ROY PETERSON
Courtesy Vancouver Sun

DAVID HITCH
Courtesy Worcester Telegram and Gazette (Mass.)

122

JAMES McCLOSKEY
Courtesy The News Leader (Va.)

NICK ANDERSON
Courtesy Houston Chronicle

RICK McKEE
Courtesy Augusta Chronicle (Ga.)

DENNIS GALVEZ
Courtesy Philippine News

Israel at 60

DANZIGER
NYTS/CWS May 8 08 (3594)

JEFF DANZIGER
Courtesy NYTS/CWS

POL GALVEZ
Courtesy Philippine News

I LOVE URANIUM

POL GALVEZ
8-13-08
PHILIPPINE NEWS
BURLINGAME, CALIF.

BOB GORRELL
Courtesy Creators Syndicate

LARRY WRIGHT
Courtesy Detroit News

MICHAEL OSBUN
Courtesy Citrus City Chronicle (Fla.)

MIKE BECKOM
Courtesy Hartsville Messenger

CLAY BENNETT
Courtesy Chattanooga Times Free Press

STEVE NEASE
Courtesy Toronto Sun

ADAM ZYGLIS
Courtesy Buffalo News

STEVE McBRIDE
Courtesy Independence Daily Reporter (Kan.)

PEDRO MOLINA
Courtesy CWS

ED STEIN
Courtesy Rocky Mountain News (Colo.)

CASTRO QUITS

THE CHANGING OF THE GUARD

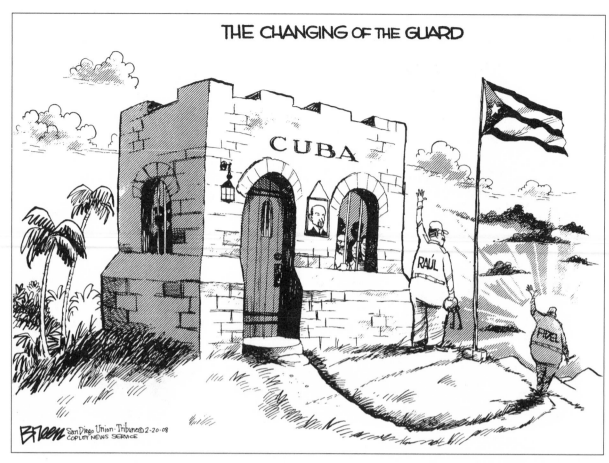

STEVE BREEN
Courtesy San Diego Union-Tribune

ED GAMBLE
Courtesy Florida Times-Union

Congress

The United States in 2008 found itself confronting a full-blown energy crisis. Congress, however, failed to decisively initiate a fix, contenting itself with finger pointing and restating its opposition to developing domestic resources.

The price of gasoline soared to $5 in some areas, prompting Republicans to call for drilling offshore and in the Arctic National Wildlife Refuge. Democrats responded by insisting that oil companies are sitting on large tracts of untapped oil reserves.

In the financial world, a flood of home mortgage foreclosures sank a growing number of financial institutions and threatened the entire economy, leaving Congress no choice but to act. Some blamed George Bush while others pointed to a lack of oversight by a Democratic-controlled Congress. Still others pointed to a government policy of encouraging home loans to financially shaky buyers through Fannie Mae and Freddie Mac. The bottom line appeared to be a trillion-dollar-plus bailout, or rescue, backed by the full faith and credit of the United States treasury.

"Earmarks," the funding of specific pet projects, remained a contentious congressional issue.

DAVID HITCH
Courtesy Worcester Telegram and Gazette (Mass.)

BOB GORRELL
Courtesy Creators Syndicate

RICHARD WALLMEYER
Courtesy Long Beach Press-Telegram (Calif.)

S.C. RAWLS
Courtesy Rockdale Citizen (Ga.)

JIM LANGE
Courtesy The Daily Oklahoman

ROB ROGERS
Courtesy Pittsburgh Post-Gazette

133

Best of Breed, 2008 Washington D.C. Kennel Club: the Democratic Congress Lap Donkey

RUSSELL HODIN
Courtesy The New Times (Calif.)

STEVE KELLEY
Courtesy The Times-Picayune (La.)

NEIL GRAHAME
Courtesy Spencer Newspapers

WORLDS APART

JIM LANGE
Courtesy The Daily Oklahoman

RICK KOLLINGER
Courtesy The Evening Sun (Md.)

STEVEN LAIT
Courtesy Oakland Tribune

MIKE LUCKOVICH
Courtesy Atlanta Journal-Constitution

MICHAEL RAMIREZ
Courtesy Investors Business Daily

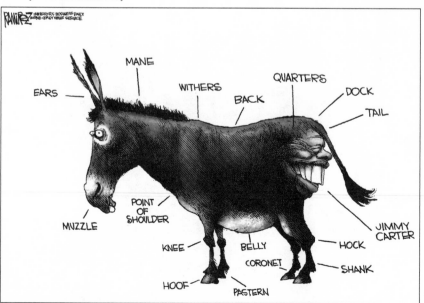

Politics

As the presidential campaign heated up, the call for change reverberated across the land. Just about every candidate promised to bring about that change, but the politics of change seemed to have reverted to politics as usual.

The Rev. Jesse Jackson was caught on an open microphone making crude comments about the candidacy of Barack Obama. An apology was quickly forthcoming.

John Edwards, who a few months before was considered a serious contender for the Democratic nomination, acknowledged having had an affair with a documentary filmmaker. His admission came after months of denying the charge to inquiring reporters.

New York Gov. Eliot Spitzer, regarded by many as a modern-day crusader for the American way, resigned after admitting to a relationship with a prostitute.

Sen. Ted Kennedy of Massachusetts was operated on for a brain tumor, and his condition appeared to be improving. Perennial presidential candidate Ralph Nader began gearing up for another run for the nation's highest office.

DANI AGUILA
Courtesy Filipino Reporter

el dani's © 5/30'08
POLITICAL MEN-agerie
NY Filipino Reporter

EDWARD 'TED' KENNEDY: "Last Liberal Lion in the US Senate"

OLD LIONS NEVER LIE; THEY JEST, LAY OVER AND PREY♪

THE RUMOR OF MY BRAIN TUMOR IS CONFIRMED; BUT I REFUSE TO BE INFIRMED!

NICK ANDERSON
Courtesy Houston Chronicle

J.D. CROWE
Courtesy Mobile Press-Register

MIKE LUCKOVICH
Courtesy Atlanta Journal-Constitution

DENNIS DRAUGHON
Courtesy The Insider (N.C.)

NATE BEELER
Courtesy Washington Examiner

MIKE PETERS
Courtesy Dayton Daily News

DICK LOCHER
Courtesy Chicago Tribune

Immigration

A 2008 immigration reform bill cosponsored by Sen. John McCain failed to pass Congress. McCain had altered his stance on immigration after a public outcry. Citizens had demanded that the porous border with Mexico be sealed before any comprehensive reform could be attempted.

Both Hillary Clinton and Barack Obama had voted in 2006 for a controversial 700-mile-long fence along the border. McCain also voted for the fence, but declared: "We need workers in this country. There are certain jobs that Americans are simply not willing to do."

The conundrum facing politicians remained how to secure the border and at the same time find the needed work force while dealing with an estimated 12 million illegal immigrants already in the country. Compounding the problem: Many businesses regard illegal immigrants as a source of cheap labor, and many politicians see them as an important future voting bloc.

EUGENE PAYNE
Courtesy Charlotte Observer

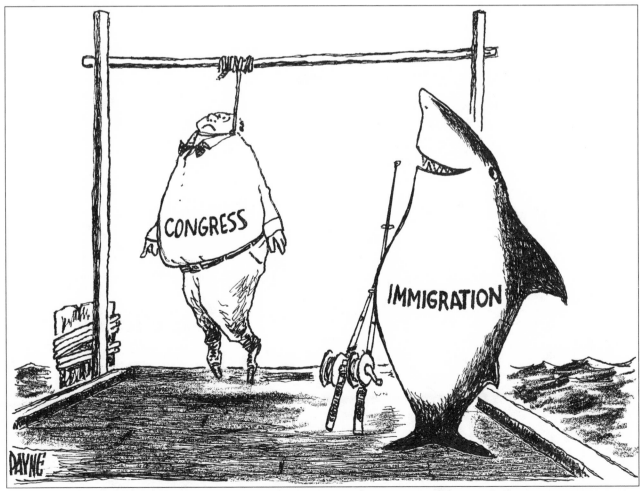

STEVE NEASE
Courtesy Toronto Sun

STEVE BREEN
Courtesy San Diego Union-Tribune

ANN CLEAVES
Courtesy Ann Cleaves

JOE HELLER
Courtesy Green Bay Press-Gazette

PETER EVANS
Courtesy The Islander News (Fla.)

MIKE BECKOM
Courtesy Hartsville Messenger

The Media

A great many observers believe that the news media is strongly biased in favor of Barack Obama, and that the bias is reflected in their reporting. Media critics pointed out, for example, that none of the networks accompanied John McCain on his trip to Iraq, but they did provide extensive live coverage of Obama's summer European excursion.

The mainstream media was also criticized for sitting on a story, eventually confirmed, detailing infidelity by Democrat John Edwards while rushing into print unfounded allegations of an affair by his Republican opponent.

Elsewhere, there were relatively few reports from Iraq, primarily because the level of violence in that country had dropped significantly after the troop surge. Obama's speech in Berlin received heavy press coverage, leading some pundits to compare it favorably to John F. Kennedy's address in the city a generation earlier.

The journalism profession lost an esteemed member with the death of Tim Russert. NBC's Washington bureau chief and moderator of "Meet the Press," Russert was a highly respected commentator on current affairs.

RICK McKEE
Courtesy Augusta Chronicle (Ga.)

WAYNE STROOT
Courtesy Hastings Tribune (Neb.)

DAVID BROWN
Courtesy Los Angeles Sentinel

JAMES McCLOSKEY
Courtesy The News Leader (Va.)

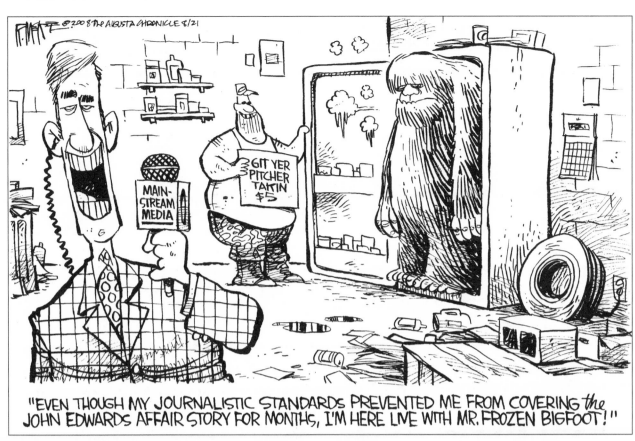

RICK McKEE
Courtesy Augusta Chronicle (Ga.)

ROB TORNOE
Courtesy rob.tornoe@potlicker.com

CHUCK ASAY
Courtesy Creators Syndicate

NEIL GRAHAME
Courtesy Spencer Newspapers

"It's an honor to meet the press, Tim."

JOHN SHERFFIUS
Courtesy Boulder Camera (Colo.)

STEVE EDWARDS
Courtesy St. Louis Journalism Review

STEPHEN TEMPLETON
Courtesy The Flathead Beacon (Mont.)

BOB GORRELL
Courtesy Creators Syndicate

DANA SUMMERS
Courtesy Orlando Sentinel

DEB MILBRATH
Courtesy CNN AAEC Website

MARK STREETER
Courtesy Savannah Morning News

LARRY KASSELL
Courtesy Silverton Appeal Tribune (Ore.)

Dude! If you're a senior, you shouldn't be eating here.

SAGE STOSSEL
Courtesy The Atlantic Monthly

BRUCE BEATTIE
Courtesy Daytona Beach News-Journal

"He died from 'Can't Afford the Copayment' disease."

Health/Education

An outbreak of salmonella in 2008 sickened hundreds of people in the United States. Officials originally placed the blame on tomatoes, but later suggested some other type of produce could have been responsible. Nevertheless, the pronouncement proved disastrous for tomato farmers, whose crops rotted on the vine and in packing plants.

Tomato losses were reported to exceed $100 million, and industry leaders called for an investigation into the government's handling of the matter.

By several measures, health care spending continues to rise at the fastest rate in history. Such spending in 2007 reached $2.3 trillion, more than four times the amount spent on national defense. Although nearly 47 million Americans are uninsured, the United States still spends more for health care than other industrialized nations, and those countries provide health insurance to all their citizens.

The nationwide problem of obesity remains a major concern, especially as it affects children.

On the education front, schools continued to try to deal with underfunding.

TIM BENSON
Courtesy Argus Leader (S.D.)

153

DARREL AKERS
Courtesy The Reporter (Calif.)

LARRY WRIGHT
Courtesy Detroit News

IRENE JOSLIN
Courtesy Brown County Democrat (Ind.)

JOSEPH HOFFECKER
Courtesy American City Business Journals

LARRY WRIGHT
Courtesy Detroit News

ANNETTE BALESTERI
Courtesy Antioch News (Calif.)

JIM DYKE
Courtesy Jefferson City News-Tribune (Mo.)

The Military

Critics say the Bush Administration has done a poor job of caring for the men and women wounded in combat in Iraq. As proof, they point to some appalling conditions uncovered during 2008 at Walter Reed National Army Medical Center.

Guards at the Guantanamo Bay Detention Camp in Cuba were accused in media reports of mistreating terrorist suspects. Since 2001, when war in Afghanistan began, 775 detainees have been housed in the camp. Of that number, 420 have been released without charge, and only one has been convicted of a crime. There have also been reports of detainees attacking their guards.

The American Civil Liberties Union has mounted a campaign to force closure of the Guantanamo facility.

Most leaders of both political parties agree that the present-day armed forces are the finest ever.

VAUGHN LARSON
Courtesy Wisconsin News-Press

157

MARK BAKER
Courtesy The Army Times

KEN VEGOTSKY
Courtesy Bucks County Courier-Times (Pa.)

BILL GARNER
Courtesy Washington Times

BOB LANG
Courtesy Rightoons.com

DENNIS DRAUGHON
Courtesy Fayetteville Observer (N.C.)

MARK BAKER
Courtesy The Army Times

JOHN AUCHTER
Courtesy Grand Rapids Business Journal

The Environment

California was hit by wildfires several times during the year. Walls of wind-whipped flames roared across tinder-dry Southern California, consuming hundreds of homes. Hundreds of thousands of residents were forced to flee.

Global warming remains a hot button issue. The Bush Administration was accused by many warming advocates of not adequately addressing the problem. The Department of Interior designated the polar bear as a species threatened with extinction because of shrinking sea ice, making it the first creature to be added to the endangered list primarily because of global warming.

The subject of air pollution attracted major attention during the 2008 Olympics in Beijing, China. Some athletes wore masks to protect themselves from the city's thick soot and smog, dangerous ozone levels, and air quality ranked among the worst in the world.

Smoking is still a hot issue. States, cities, universities, and businesses continued to devise measures to clamp down on the practice.

The Supreme Court reduced punitive damages for the 1989 *Exxon Valdez* oil spill to $507.5 million.

JOHN SHERFFIUS
Courtesy Boulder Camera (Colo.)

GEORGE DANBY
Courtesy Bangor Daily News

RICHARD WALLMEYER
Courtesy Long Beach Press-Telegram (Calif.)

PETER DUNLAP-SHOHL
Courtesy Anchorage Daily News

MILT PRIGGEE
Courtesy Puget Sound Business Journal

STEVE GREENBERG
Courtesy Ventura County Star

RANDY BISH
Courtesy Tribune-Review (Pa.)

DENNIS GALVEZ
Courtesy Philippine News

CHUCK LEGGE
Courtesy The Frontiersman (Alaska)

JESSE SPRINGER
Courtesy Eugene Register-Guard (Ore.)

PAUL CONRAD
Courtesy Tribune Media Services

RUSSELL HODIN
Courtesy The New Times (Calif.)

DOUG REGALIA
Courtesy Contra Costa Times (Calif.)

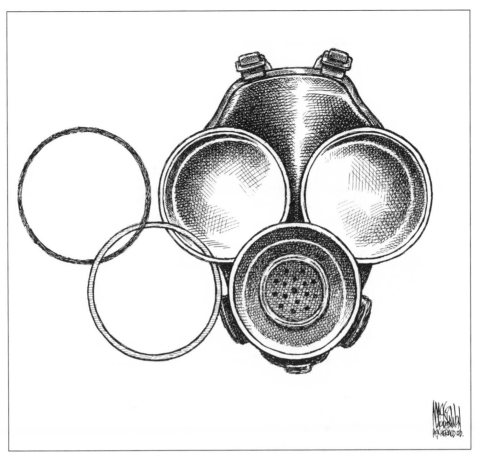

BRUCE MacKINNON
Courtesy Halifax Herald (Canada)

WALT HANDELSMAN
Courtesy Newsday

RICHARD WALLMEYER
Courtesy Long Beach Press-Telegram (Calif.)

JOE HELLER
Courtesy Green Bay Press-Gazette

Air Travel

2008 was a difficult year for airlines. Continental cut 3,000 jobs and reduced capacity by 11 percent, citing record fuel costs that have pushed the industry into its worst crisis since 2001.

Southwest Airlines grounded 43 planes to determine if they were structurally strong enough to carry passengers after admitting it had missed required inspections for cracks in some planes. The airline faces a $10.2 million civil penalty for continuing to fly almost 50 planes after the airline informed regulators of the lapse.

American Airlines canceled more than 1,000 flights to repair faulty wiring that could cause a short circuit or even a fire and explosion.

Problems such as these continue to cause long lines at ticket counters and make flying even more stressful than usual.

DAVID DONAR
Courtesy Macomb Daily (Miss.)

BILL WHITEHEAD
Courtesy Kansas City Business Journal

JOSEPH HOFFECKER
Courtesy American City Business Journals

STEVE KELLEY
Courtesy The Times-Picayune (La.)

MILT PRIGGEE
Courtesy Puget Sound Business Journal

JON RICHARDS
Courtesy Albuquerque Journal North

WAYNE STAYSKAL
Courtesy Tribune Media Services

STAN BURDICK
Courtesy Lake Champlain Weekly

ED GAMBLE
Courtesy Florida Times-Union

WAYNE STAYSKAL
Courtesy Tribune Media Services

STEVE KELLEY
Courtesy The Times-Picayune (La.)

Society

California's Supreme Court declared that gay couples in the state are free to marry—a victory for the gay rights movement that was greeted with tears, hugs, kisses, and instant proposals of matrimony. Religious and social conservatives immediately began a campaign to place a constitutional amendment on the ballot to undo the ruling.

The proliferation of cell phones has made the nation's roadways more dangerous as more and more drivers are distracted by conversations and text messaging.

Soaring gasoline prices made life more difficult for millions of Americans, pushing up the cost of living, reducing driving, and causing many people to curtail or cancel vacations. Home foreclosures continued to rise, adding to homeowner woes.

ANNETTE BALESTERI
Courtesy Antioch News (Calif.)

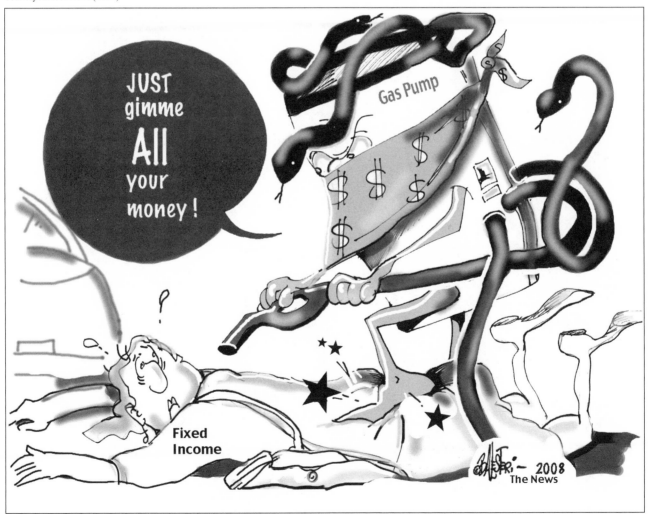

JACK JURDEN
Courtesy Wilmington News-Journal

JIM BORGMAN
Courtesy Cincinnati Enquirer

TONY BAYER
Courtesy The News Dispatch (Ind.)

WALT HANDELSMAN
Courtesy Newsday

PAUL FELL
Courtesy Artizans Syndicate

STEVE KELLEY
Courtesy The Times-Picayune (La.)

BILL WHITEHEAD
Courtesy Kansas City Business Journal

DOUGLAS MacGREGOR
Courtesy Fort Myers News-Press

Who Are Ya Gonna Believe?

JEFF DANZIGER
Courtesy NYTS/CWS

JOE HELLER
Courtesy Green Bay Press-Gazette

PETER EVANS
Courtesy The Islander News (Fla.)

CHUCK ASAY
Courtesy Creators Syndicate

RICKY NOBILE
Courtesy nobilericky@aol.com

BRUCE BEATTIE
Courtesy Daytona Beach News-Journal

"Nice to know America's still the world's leader in SOMETHING!"

DAVE SATTLER
Courtesy LaFayette Journal-Courier (Ind.)

CHUCK ASAY
Courtesy Creators Syndicate

GARY VARVEL
Courtesy Indianapolis Star

182

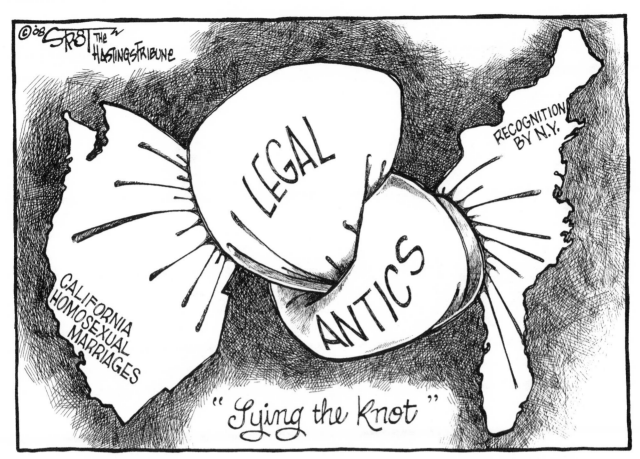

WAYNE STROOT
Courtesy Hastings Tribune (Neb.)

CLAY BENNETT
Courtesy Chattanooga Times Free Press

TIM HARTMAN
Courtesy Beaver County Times (Pa.)

RANDY BISH
Courtesy Tribune-Review (Pa.)

Sports

Michael Phelps swam into history at the summer Olympics in Beijing, winning his 10th and 11th career gold medals and setting five new world records. Several of the Chinese participants were reportedly found to be underage. Protestors in Beijing against China's iron rule in Tibet were given short shrift.

Former Sen. George Mitchell in 2008 issued a report on the use of performance-enhancing drugs in sports. In all, 89 players were named, including free agent Roger Clemens. Barry Bonds was suspected of steroid abuse.

Green Bay Packers quarterback Brett Favre announced his retirement, then changed his mind and signed with another team. Tiger Woods won the U.S. Open while recovering from surgery, and Michael Vick was sentenced for his participation in illegal dog fighting.

Big Brown won the Kentucky Derby but the filly Eight Belles suffered a fall on the track, breaking both ankles. She was euthanized on the spot, and animal rights activists quickly expressed outrage.

THEO MOUDAKIS
Courtesy Toronto Star

185

JOHN RILEY
Courtesy johnrileycartoons.com

MIKE PETERS
Courtesy Dayton Daily News

TOM STIGLICH
Courtesy Northeast Times (Pa.)

PEDRO MOLINA
Courtesy CWS

JOE HELLER
Courtesy Green Bay Press-Gazette

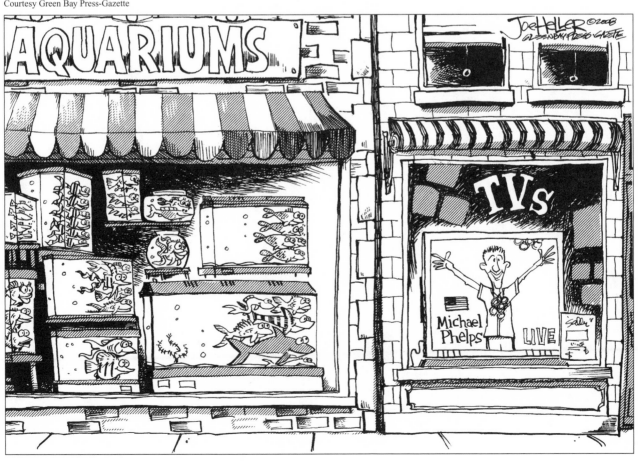

RICKY NOBILE
Courtesy nobilericky@aol.com

GUY BADEAUX
Courtesy Le Droit (Canada)

S.C. RAWLS
Courtesy Rockdale Citizen (Ga.)

CHRIS BRITT
Courtesy State Journal-Register (Ill.)

JACK HIGGINS
Courtesy Chicago Sun-Times

189

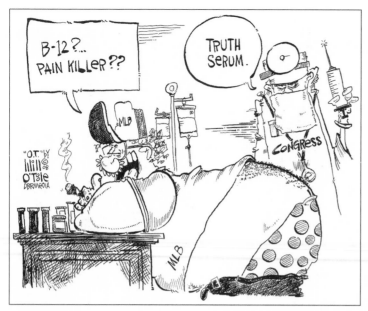

WILL O'TOOLE
Courtesy DBR Media

CHARLIE HALL
Courtesy Rhode Island News Group

LINDA BOILEAU
Courtesy Frankfort State Journal (Ky.)

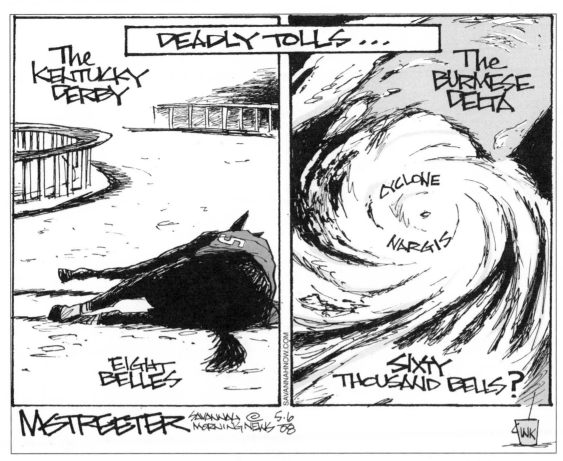

MARK STREETER
Courtesy Savannah Morning News

PHIL HANDS
Courtesy Wisconsin State Journal

WILL O'TOOLE
Courtesy DBR Media

PAUL FELL
Courtesy Artizans Syndicate

JOHN TREVER
Courtesy Albuquerque Journal

192

WILL O'TOOLE
Courtesy DBR Media

TIM JACKSON
Courtesy Chicago Defender

STEVE LINDSTROM
Courtesy Duluth News-Tribune

TIM BENSON
Courtesy Argus Leader (S.D.)

... and Other Issues

With the cost of oil going through the roof, offshore drilling became an even more attractive issue for Republicans, who have long supported more exploration. Many Democrats, feeling pressure from constituents weary of ever-soaring gasoline prices, began to rethink their opposition to increased domestic energy production.

The energy crisis sparked a separate debate over the use of corn to make ethanol. The move raised the price of corn, which was good for farmers, but proved to be a harsh blow for developing countries trying to feed their populations.

The Pentagon charged six detainees at Guantanamo Bay with murder and war crimes in connection with the September 11 attacks. Officials will seek the death penalty in what would be the first capital trials under the terrorism-era military tribunal system.

The Supreme Court, in its first major pronouncement on gun rights, ruled that Americans have a constitutional right to own firearms for self-defense in their homes. Among notables who died in 2008 were William F. Buckley, television commentator Tim Russert, former Sen. Jesse Helms, and actor George Carlin.

And the debate between evolutionists and creationists continued.

JOHN TREVER
Courtesy Albuquerque Journal

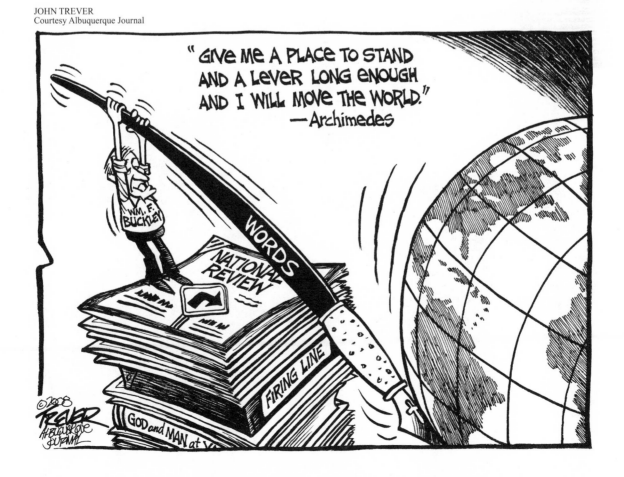

195

STEVE BREEN
Courtesy San Diego Union-Tribune

ROY PETERSON
Courtesy Vancouver Sun

JIM MORIN
Courtesy Miami Herald

JEFF DANZIGER
Courtesy NYTS/CWS

ADAM ZYGLIS
Courtesy Buffalo News

JIM MORIN
Courtesy Miami Herald

TOM STIGLICH
Courtesy Northeast Times (Pa.)

JOHN TREVER
Courtesy Albuquerque Journal

198

J.R. ROSE
Courtesy Byrd Newspapers of Virginia

ROSS GOSSE
Courtesy Editoons.iNCk

MATT BORS
Courtesy UFS, Inc.

CHARLIE HALL
Courtesy Rhode Island News Group

JOHN COLE
Courtesy Scranton Times-Tribune

JAKE FULLER
Courtesy Gainesville Sun

SCOTT STANTIS
Courtesy Birmingham News

ELIZABETH BRICQUET
Courtesy Kingsport Times-News (Tenn.)

SCOTT STANTIS
Courtesy Birmingham News

Past Award Winners

PULITZER PRIZE

1922—Rollin Kirby, New York World
1923—No award given
1924—J.N. Darling, New York Herald-Tribune
1925—Rollin Kirby, New York World
1926—D.R. Fitzpatrick, St. Louis Post-Dispatch
1927—Nelson Harding, Brooklyn Eagle
1928—Nelson Harding, Brooklyn Eagle
1929—Rollin Kirby, New York World
1930—Charles Macauley, Brooklyn Eagle
1931—Edmund Duffy, Baltimore Sun
1932—John T. McCutcheon, Chicago Tribune
1933—H.M. Talburt, Washington Daily News
1934—Edmund Duffy, Baltimore Sun
1935—Ross A. Lewis, Milwaukee Journal
1936—No award given
1937—C.D. Batchelor, New York Daily News
1938—Vaughn Shoemaker, Chicago Daily News
1939—Charles G. Werner, Daily Oklahoman
1940—Edmund Duffy, Baltimore Sun
1941—Jacob Burck, Chicago Times
1942—Herbert L. Block, NEA
1943—Jay N. Darling, New York Herald-Tribune
1944—Clifford K. Berryman, Washington Star
1945—Bill Mauldin, United Features Syndicate
1946—Bruce Russell, Los Angeles Times
1947—Vaughn Shoemaker, Chicago Daily News
1948—Reuben L. ("Rube") Goldberg, New York Sun
1949—Lute Pease, Newark Evening News
1950—James T. Berryman, Washington Star
1951—Reginald W. Manning, Arizona Republic
1952—Fred L. Packer, New York Mirror
1953—Edward D. Kuekes, Cleveland Plain Dealer
1954—Herbert L. Block, Washington Post
1955—Daniel R. Fitzpatrick, St. Louis Post-Dispatch
1956—Robert York, Louisville Times
1957—Tom Little, Nashville Tennessean
1958—Bruce M. Shanks, Buffalo Evening News
1959—Bill Mauldin, St. Louis Post-Dispatch
1960—No award given
1961—Carey Orr, Chicago Tribune
1962—Edmund S. Valtman, Hartford Times
1963—Frank Miller, Des Moines Register
1964—Paul Conrad, Denver Post
1965—No award given
1966—Don Wright, Miami News
1967—Patrick B. Oliphant, Denver Post
1968—Eugene Gray Payne, Charlotte Observer
1969—John Fischetti, Chicago Daily News
1970—Thomas F. Darcy, Newsday
1971—Paul Conrad, Los Angeles Times
1972—Jeffrey K. MacNelly, Richmond News Leader
1973—No award given
1974—Paul Szep, Boston Globe
1975—Garry Trudeau, Universal Press Syndicate
1976—Tony Auth, Philadelphia Enquirer

1977—Paul Szep, Boston Globe
1978—Jeff MacNelly, Richmond News Leader
1979—Herbert Block, Washington Post
1980—Don Wright, Miami News
1981—Mike Peters, Dayton Daily News
1982—Ben Sargent, Austin American-Statesman
1983—Dick Locher, Chicago Tribune
1984—Paul Conrad, Los Angeles Times
1985—Jeff MacNelly, Chicago Tribune
1986—Jules Feiffer, Universal Press Syndicate
1987—Berke Breathed, Washington Post Writers Group
1988—Doug Marlette, Atlanta Constitution
1989—Jack Higgins, Chicago Sun-Times
1990—Tom Toles, Buffalo News
1991—Jim Borgman, Cincinnati Enquirer
1992—Signe Wilkinson, Philadelphia Daily News
1993—Steve Benson, Arizona Republic
1994—Michael Ramirez, Memphis Commercial Appeal
1995—Mike Luckovich, Atlanta Constitution
1996—Jim Morin, Miami Herald
1997—Walt Handelsman, New Orleans Times-Picayune
1998—Steve Breen, Asbury Park Press
1999—David Horsey, Seattle Post-Intelligencer
2000—Joel Pett, Lexington Herald-Leader
2001—Ann Telnaes, Tribune Media Services
2002—Clay Bennett, Christian Science Monitor
2003—David Horsey, Seattle Post-Intelligencer
2004—Matt Davies, The Journal News
2005—Nick Anderson, Louisville Courier-Journal
2006—Mike Luckovich, Atlanta Journal-Constitution
2007—Walt Handelsman, Newsday
2008—Michael Ramirez, Investors Business Daily

SIGMA DELTA CHI AWARD

1942—Jacob Burck, Chicago Times
1943—Charles Werner, Chicago Sun
1944—Henry Barrow, Associated Press
1945—Reuben L. Goldberg, New York Sun
1946—Dorman H. Smith, NEA
1947—Bruce Russell, Los Angeles Times
1948—Herbert Block, Washington Post
1949—Herbert Block, Washington Post
1950—Bruce Russell, Los Angeles Times
1951—Herbert Block, Washington Post and
        Bruce Russell, Los Angeles Times
1952—Cecil Jensen, Chicago Daily News
1953—John Fischetti, NEA
1954—Calvin Alley, Memphis Commercial Appeal
1955—John Fischetti, NEA
1956—Herbert Block, Washington Post
1957—Scott Long, Minneapolis Tribune
1958—Clifford H. Baldowski, Atlanta Constitution
1959—Charles G. Brooks, Birmingham News
1960—Dan Dowling, New York Herald-Tribune
1961—Frank Interlandi, Des Moines Register

PAST AWARD WINNERS

1962—Paul Conrad, Denver Post
1963—William Mauldin, Chicago Sun-Times
1964—Charles Bissell, Nashville Tennessean
1965—Roy Justus, Minneapolis Star
1966—Patrick Oliphant, Denver Post
1967—Eugene Payne, Charlotte Observer
1968—Paul Conrad, Los Angeles Times
1969—William Mauldin, Chicago Sun-Times
1970—Paul Conrad, Los Angeles Times
1971—Hugh Haynie, Louisville Courier-Journal
1972—William Mauldin, Chicago Sun-Times
1973—Paul Szep, Boston Globe
1974—Mike Peters, Dayton Daily News
1975—Tony Auth, Philadelphia Enquirer
1976—Paul Szep, Boston Globe
1977—Don Wright, Miami News
1978—Jim Borgman, Cincinnati Enquirer
1979—John P. Trever, Albuquerque Journal
1980—Paul Conrad, Los Angeles Times
1981—Paul Conrad, Los Angeles Times
1982—Dick Locher, Chicago Tribune
1983—Rob Lawlor, Philadelphia Daily News
1984—Mike Lane, Baltimore Evening Sun

1985—Doug Marlette, Charlotte Observer
1986—Mike Keefe, Denver Post
1987—Paul Conrad, Los Angeles Times
1988—Jack Higgins, Chicago Sun-Times
1989—Don Wright, Palm Beach Post
1990—Jeff MacNelly, Chicago Tribune
1991—Walt Handelsman, New Orleans Times-Picayune
1992—Robert Ariail, Columbia State
1993—Herbert Block, Washington Post
1994—Jim Borgman, Cincinnati Enquirer
1995—Michael Ramirez, Memphis Commercial Appeal
1996—Paul Conrad, Los Angeles Times
1997—Michael Ramirez, Los Angeles Times
1998—Jack Higgins, Chicago Sun-Times
1999—Mike Thompson, Detroit Free Press
2000—Nick Anderson, Louisville Courier-Journal
2001—Clay Bennett, Christian Science Monitor
2002—Mike Thompson, Detroit Free Press
2003—Steve Sack, Minneapolis Star-Tribune
2004—John Sherffius, jsherffius@aol.com
2005—Mike Luckovich, Atlanta Journal-Constitution
2006—Mike Lester, Rome News-Tribune
2007—Michael Ramirez, Investors Business Daily

Index of Cartoonists

INDEX OF CARTOONISTS